REACH, GATHER, GROW
IN EPHESIANS

DR. RANDY T. JOHNSON

WITH CONTRIBUTIONS FROM:

CAMERON ALDRICH	ALYSSA FAIRSE	JILL OSMON
NOBLE BAIRD	MELVIN FRICK	PHILIP PIASECKI
JASMYN BICKNELL	DEBBIE GABBARA	MARK PITTENGER
PATRICK BICKNELL	GRANT GRIMES	RICH SAWICKI
JOHN CARTER	LORENA HABER	JOSH THAYER
CALEB COMBS	MITCHELL HOLMES	KARSEN THEEDE
JOSH COMBS	ZACH HONNEN	ROY TOWNSEND
SIERRA COMBS	DAVID HUDGENS	JEANNIE YATES
JUSTIN DEAN	CHUCK LINDSEY	

DESIGNED BY LORENA HABER
FORMATTED BY SHAWNA JOHNSON

Reach, Gather, Grow, in Ephesians

Copyright © 2025 by The River Church

Published by The River Church
    8393 E. Holly Rd.
    Holly, MI 48442

No part of this book may be reproduced or transmitted in any form or by any means, electronic or mechanical, including photocopying, recording or by any information storage and retrieval system, without the written permission of The River Church. Inquiries should be sent to the publisher. All rights reserved.

First Edition, January 2025

Printed in the United States of America

Scripture quotations are from the ESV® Bible (The Holy Bible, English Standard Version®), copyright © 2001 by Crossway, a publishing ministry of Good News Publishers. Used by permission. All rights reserved. The ESV text may not be quoted in any publication made available to the public by a Creative Commons license. The ESV may not be translated in whole or in part into any other language. The Holy Bible, English Standard Version®, is adapted from the Revised Standard Version of the Bible, copyright Division of Christian Education of the National Council of the Churches of Christ in the U.S.A.

THE RIVER CHURCH
REACH | GATHER | GROW

CONTENTS

09	**LESSON ONE • REACH**
19	Devotion 1: Over Our Dead Bodies
21	Devotion 2: Free Gift
23	Devotion 3: What is the Gospel?
27	Devotion 4: Reach the World
29	Devotion 5: I Got It
31	Devotion 6: But God
35	**LESSON TWO • GATHER**
43	Devotion 1: Standing Strong Together
45	Devotion 2: Participation Award
47	Devotion 3: Gathering as the Church
49	Devotion 4: Make a Joyful Noise!
51	Devotion 5: Unity
53	Devotion 6: Everyone is Needed
57	**LESSON THREE • GROW**
65	Devotion 1: Talk the Talk
67	Devotion 2: Words are Hard!
69	Devotion 3: Growing in Difficulty
71	Devotion 4: Imitators of Christ
73	Devotion 5: Praying for Growth
75	Devotion 6: Words Matter
79	**LESSON FOUR • GIVING**
87	Devotion 1: "To Join Him in His Work"
89	Devotion 2: Grumbling to Gratitude
91	Devotion 3: Likeness of the Father
93	Devotion 4: A Boy's Lunch
95	Devotion 5: Smell Test
97	Devotion 6: The Gift of Service
101	**THE BOOK OF EPHESIANS**

PREFACE

In Matthew 28:19-20, Jesus commands the mission for the church, **"Go therefore and make disciples of all nations, baptizing them in the name of the Father and of the Son and of the Holy Spirit, teaching them to observe all that I have commanded you. And behold, I am with you always, to the end of the age."** Some of Jesus' last words on Earth were for His followers to spread the Gospel, gather together for worship, and grow together in spiritual maturity.

In the book of Ephesians, Paul follows these same guidelines as he directs the church in Ephesus to Reach, Gather, and Grow. It is challenging and at the same time comforting to see the several examples in Ephesians of how Paul strives to implement Jesus' mission for His church.

"Reach, Gather, Grow, in Ephesians" contains four study guides for personal or group discussion and twenty-four devotions for further insight. *"Reach, Gather, Grow, in Ephesians"* will remind you of the importance of your role as part of the church and will help you view the book of Ephesians from a new and fresh perspective.

LESSON ONE

REACH

PASTOR NOBLE BAIRD

In Matthew 28:19-20, Jesus shares His final commission with His disciples and followers. However, it is more than just a final thought and command. Jesus intentionally shares His desire for what His followers ought to do with the life-changing teachings and truth of His Gospel, which they were all taught by Him. This final calling was not taken lightly. Jesus entrusted this call of sharing His Gospel, to be led by the Spirit, to abandon their past lives and selfish desires, to total surrender and obedience of sharing the truth of Jesus' life, death for our sins, and His glorious resurrection. So, what is the first step in Christ's call and desire for their lives? *"Go."* Jesus tells His disciples and followers to take a true step in obedience. It is something that they can objectively accomplish and follow through on: *"Go."*

1. When was the last time that someone told or asked you to go do something for them?

   _____
   _____
   _____

2. What was your response? Did you want to actually do that? Why?

   _____
   _____
   _____

In the book of Ephesians, Paul is writing to the church in Ephesus, and as he always does, he is encouraging them and imparting doctrinal truth to these new churches, but he also challenges and lovingly rebukes some of their actions. It is believed that this is a "prison epistle," meaning that it was written during one of Paul's imprisonments, potentially in Rome. In Ephesians 2:1-10, he writes, *"And you were dead in the trespasses and sins in which you once walked, following the course of this world, following the prince of the power of the air, the spirit that is now at work in the sons of disobedience - among whom we all once lived in the passions of our flesh, carrying out the desires of the body and the mind, and were by nature children of wrath, like the rest of mankind. But God, being rich in mercy, because of the great love with which he loved us, even when we were dead in our trespasses, made us alive together with Christ - by grace, you have been saved - and raised us up with him and seated us with him in the heavenly places in Christ Jesus, so that in the coming ages he might show the immeasurable riches of his grace in kindness toward us in Christ Jesus. For by grace you have been saved through faith. And this is not your own doing; it is the gift of God, not a result of works, so that no one may boast. For we are his workmanship, created in Christ Jesus for good works, which God prepared beforehand, that we should walk in them."*

First, Paul sets the context and foundational understanding of the spiritual and eternal trajectory of the world. He writes in verses 1-3 that everyone in this world is spiritually dead in our trespasses and sins. Furthermore, the fleshly desires of this world and all who live in it are canted towards selfishness, disobedience, and a stranglehold by Satan. This is the unfortunate true reality of sin. Romans 3:23 reminds us, just as here in Ephesians 2, **"For all have sinned and fall short of the glory of God."** This is what we all must accept and understand: that at the core of our lives and who we are is totally sinful. Simply put, complete inability to do good and complete separation from God.

3. Do you remember what your life was like before Christ? What were some of the characteristics that described what led you and your desires?

_____

_____

_____

4. Did you ever feel that you were good enough or able to attain Heaven through yourself alone? Why? What did that look like?

_____
_____
_____

Continuing on in verse 4, Paul makes an incredible statement, **"But God."** That is definitely a daily, minute-by-minute reminder that we can all use! Honestly, maybe some of us need to tattoo that on our wrist to simply remember the truth of what the Lord did for us through Jesus. Paul writes in verses 4-7 how God poured out His mercy and love upon us. Now, he does not say that the Lord is doing this after we are baptized, after we have cleaned our lives up and "feel" we can walk into church, or even after we have read the whole Bible! No, Paul makes it clear that the Lord shows us His mercy and His great love for us while we are still dead in our sins. Why? It is because that is the true, loving, and redemptive power of Christ's death on the cross for us and our sins. Then Paul makes such an important statement in verse 5, sharing how the merciful grace of the Lord is received simply through faith in Jesus Christ. This faith is in Christ's death for our sins, that He was buried, and that He gloriously resurrected on the third day. That is where our faith and assurance of salvation must lie.

5. Can you think of a time in your life when you truly had no answers and felt there was no way out, **"But God"** stepped in? When was that? What did that look like? How did you respond?

_____
_____
_____

6. Have you forgotten those moments? Why do we allow new hardships or issues to change what we fundamentally know about God's character?

_____
_____
_____

Grace. What an incredible word, which is both an action and a gift that we, as followers of Christ, have received from God. That is what Paul reminds us in verse 8. The Lord showed us the action of His grace by sending Jesus to die on the cross for our sins. Jesus paid the ultimate price to restore the brokenness and disconnection between us and God. Then, that grace was given to our world at no cost. It is completely free! However, the caveat is that we must confess and believe in Jesus Christ as our Lord and Savior. Paul declares this in Romans 10:9. Then, Paul gives a humble reminder for all of us as followers of Christ. In verse 9, he writes that this gift of grace is truly a gift. As a gift, no one is able to work for or attain through any good works. Why? It is to keep us all humbly focused on the true finishing work of Jesus Christ.

Humility is so essential to our walk with the Lord. We must remember to check our hearts, minds, and actions daily so that they are reflective of a humble person saved by the grace of the Lord. We are called even to mimic Christ in His example of humility in Philippians 2:1-11. Christ laid out, by the example of His life, how we ought to humbly act and serve in all we do. Again, the reason is not for selfish gain or ambition but for the opportunity to share the amazing message of the Gospel with a world that is lost, broken, and stuck in sin.

7. What does the grace of the Lord mean to you and your walk with Christ?

_____
_____
_____

8. In what ways have you acted humbly, and in what ways have you missed the mark in humility when it comes to the good works that the Lord uses you for? Why is it so difficult for us, as followers of Christ, to remain humble?

_____
_____
_____

Finally, in verse 10, Paul really brings this whole passage back to the focus of our response to an action. Paul says that we are the Lord's workmanship. Wow! Did you read verse 10? The Creator of Heaven and Earth took precious intentional time to uniquely create you and me. We are His workmanship. There is nothing and no one in this world who can change that truth! I do not know what is going on in your life right now or what season you may be in, but I hope, at the very least, you are encouraged to know how loved you are by our Heavenly Father and that you were created for a purpose! What is that purpose? Paul tells us that we are created to do good works through the name and power of Jesus Christ. Once we accept Jesus as our Savior, our life is drastically changed, and the trajectory of our life is no longer focused on self, but refocused on good work for the Lord. It is work.

It is easy as followers of Christ to be on fire once we accept Christ and everything is new and fresh. However, life can happen, and what was once the priority of our walk with Christ begins to take a backseat when we slide into neutral. We coast. Yet, Paul echoes Christ's directive in Matthew 28:19, stating that we must **"Go."** We are His workmanship, created in Christ, to walk boldly in obedience to the Lord. So, when we talk about Reach as a church, it is my hope and desire that, as followers of Christ, we would not throw it into neutral. I hope and pray that we as a body would truly understand the words Paul is sharing here in Ephesians 2:1-10. The message is that we will never forget how imperfect and sinful we are. The Lord, in His grace and love for us, sent His Son, Jesus, and that it is only through Christ's sacrifice and resurrection we have been reconciled to our Father, and finally that we have been called to the action of Gospel work!

9. Who reached into your life and helped plant the seed of the Gospel?

_____
_____
_____

10. What will you do this week to **"Go"**? What will you do this month? What will you do this year to take it out of neutral and **"Go"**?

_____
_____
_____

NOTES

OVER OUR DEAD BODIES
DEVOTION #1 - PASTOR PATRICK BICKNELL

There is a quote that I heard a couple of years ago that often runs through my head. It is by the late, great pastor Charles Spurgeon. He said, "If sinners be damned, at least let them leap to Hell over our dead bodies. And if they perish, let them perish with our arms wrapped about their knees, imploring them to stay. If Hell must be filled, let it be filled in the teeth of our exertions, and let not one go unwarned and unprayed for." This is one of those quotes that, at least for me, makes me wish I was as smart as some people to come up with something as good as this. In all seriousness, though, I think this quote sums up perfectly what our urgency in reaching the world should be.

As we are going through our Reach, Gather, Grow series again, it can be easy for us to dismiss these lessons and think we do not need to pay attention because we might have heard this series preached a million times now. I want to plead with you not to do that. Pay attention and be motivated again to fulfill our mission as the church. Beginning in Ephesians chapter 2, Paul lays out the condition of fallen man by saying in verse 1, **"And you were once dead in your trespasses and sins."** He continues in verse 3, saying, **"Among whom we all once lived in the passions of our flesh, carrying out the desires of the body and the mind and were by nature children of wrath."** This is the desperate state all of us were in before the grace of God came into our lives. This is the desperate state that everyone in the world is in if they have not surrendered to the Lord Jesus and put their faith in Him as Savior. The only way they can be saved from this desperate state is through the Good News that all of us now have.

I heard it said before like this, "If you had the cure to cancer you would be telling everyone about it and going into every hospital to make sure all cancer patients get healed. Yet, as a Christian, you have something greater, you have the greatest cure for the greatest disease in this world. What are you doing to bring that cure to people?" This is the challenge all of us should have. We have the only cure that can save people from their desperate state. We need to have the urgency that men like Charles Spurgeon had. To go back to his quote, "If people are going to go to be damned, at least let them leap to Hell over our dead bodies."

FREE GIFT
DEVOTION #2 - DR. RANDY T. JOHNSON

Whenever I wrap a gift, I double check to make sure the price tag has been removed. Often after wrapping it, I doubt myself wondering if I somehow missed a less obvious sticker. I do not want them to see the price tag. I do not expect them to pay for it. It is a gift. It is free. I can even print a gift receipt which does not list the price. Since it is a gift, it is free.

As we focus on Reach in Ephesians, Paul is very clear in Ephesians 2:8-9, **"For by grace you have been saved through faith. And this is not your own doing; it is the gift of God, not a result of works, so that no one may boast."** Paul references the concept of being **"saved"** as a **"gift of God."** Since our salvation is a gift, it is free. We cannot buy or earn it. This passage is a little redundant. The phrase **"gift of God"** is sandwiched between two related phrases. It says that it is not of our own doings and not because of our work. Paul wants to make sure we get the point.

Ephesians is not the only place Paul mentions that our salvation is a **"gift of God."** Romans 6:23 says, **"For the wages of sin is death, but the free gift of God is eternal life in Christ Jesus our Lord."** As if the concept of **"gift"** is not clear enough by itself, he calls our salvation and eternal life a **"free gift."** Paul wants to make sure everyone understands this truth.

Most believers know Romans 3:23, **"For all have sinned and fall short of the glory of God."** However, we often miss the next verse. Romans 3:24 says, **"And are justified by his grace as a gift, through the redemption that is in Christ Jesus."** After describing our fallen state, Paul gives hope in the form of a gift.

Actually, Paul references our salvation using the word *"gift"* twelve times in Romans. Our English translations reference this salvation as a *"free gift"* in six of those times. Romans 5:15 says, *"But the free gift is not like the trespass. For if many died through one man's trespass, much more have the grace of God and the free gift by the grace of that one man Jesus Christ abounded for many."*

Charles Spurgeon said it this way, "Salvation is all grace, which means, free, gratis, for nothing." Therefore, we should celebrate with 2 Corinthians 9:15, *"Thanks be to God for his inexpressible gift!"*

WHAT IS THE GOSPEL?
DEVOTION #3 - PASTOR JOHN CARTER

If you have been to church any length of time you will hear the word "Gospel" used at some point. What exactly is the Gospel? Often the description attached to the Gospel is the phrase "Good News." This passage is as good a place as any to understand the Gospel or the Good News that the Bible is so eager to reveal to you.

Ephesians 2:1–10 says, *"And you were dead in the trespasses and sins in which you once walked, following the course of this world, following the prince of the power of the air, the spirit that is now at work in the sons of disobedience - among whom we all once lived in the passions of our flesh, carrying out the desires of the body and the mind, and were by nature children of wrath, like the rest of mankind. But God, being rich in mercy, because of the great love with which he loved us, even when we were dead in our trespasses, made us alive together with Christ - by grace you have been saved - and raised us up with him and seated us with him in the heavenly places in Christ Jesus, so that in the coming ages he might show the immeasurable riches of his grace in kindness toward us in Christ Jesus. For by grace you have been saved through faith. And this is not your own doing; it is the gift of God, not a result of works, so that no one may boast. For we are his workmanship, created in Christ Jesus for good works, which God prepared beforehand, that we should walk in them."*

It is important to understand that Paul is speaking to a body of believers in this book. They, by all means, should have known and understood what the Gospel is. Paul lays it out clearly so that there is no misunderstanding. They should not be thinking that maybe it is this or maybe it is that. He takes all the ambiguity out of it so the meaning and understanding of the Gospel is very clear.

Paul tells us the bad news before the good news when he says, "We were dead!" We were not just dead in a spiritual sense, but dead in every literal meaning of the word. Our goose was cooked. It was the end of the road. This position we find ourselves in (being dead) is linked to the actions we find ourselves following. It is the actions of the world, actions of the **"prince of the power of the air"** (aka the devil), and the actions or works of **"the sons of disobedience."** This action looks like (as Paul describes) passions of the flesh, the body, and the mind, and acting like angry children. It is pretty much just the way everybody humanly responds. In one phrase, we are prideful, arrogant, and selfish.

No one wants to admit this because of the obvious: who would actually admit to being arrogant, selfish, and full of pride? I know this is really hard news to hear. It is honestly some of the worst kind of news a person can listen to. This is not how I want to be known and not how I want to be characterized. If this is where the story of humanity ends, if this is where my own story ends, then we have no hope. What is the point if this is where we all find ourselves? There are two wonderful words that follow after the bad news, **"But God."**

Because of who God is (not who I am), His character (not my character), and His great love for me (not my love for Him), even when I was dead, full of pride, arrogant, and selfish, there is hope. While I was following the things of the world and the devil; God was still there. While I was acting in my flesh, pursuing the desires of my body, consumed with self in my mind, and being in disobedience to God; He made a way for me not to be dead. It was through His Son.

You see, the Good News (aka the Gospel) is all about the opposite of me. It is all about God's mercy, His love, His kindness, His immeasurable riches towards us, and Him making us alive together with Christ. It is something we receive as a gift. I do not have to pay Him back; it is not a loan. It is not a temporary idea. It is not something I did or can brag about. It is all God. It is generally at this moment that I cannot withhold the tears in my eyes because I truly understand this. If you do not understand this, I pray you will reach out to someone who can walk you through the Good News. If you do understand this, I pray you will be bold in sharing it with others. Without the Good News of Jesus, the work that is before us as a church is meaningless. Without the Gospel, the things that were prepared beforehand, the things we are to walk in (the good works) are just ashes.

REACH THE WORLD
DEVOTION #4 - JASMYN BICKNELL

"And you were dead in the trespasses and sins in which you once walked, following the course of this world, following the prince of the power of the air, the spirit that is now at work in the sons of disobedience - among whom we all once lived in the passions of our flesh, carrying out the desires of the body and the mind, and were by nature children of wrath, like the rest of mankind." Ephesians 2:1-3

"For by grace you have been saved through faith. And this is not your own doing; it is the gift of God, not a result of works, so that no one may boast." Ephesians 2:8-9

As Ephesians says in chapter 2, we were once dead; we followed what the world said was right and did whatever we wanted. Paul reminds us that we have been saved by the grace of God, and our faith in Him has granted us eternal life. However, this is not something that we have earned by "being good." In fact, we are the complete opposite of good. We have never once done something to deserve the freedom that the Lord has given us, and we never will. It is by His unconditional love and forgiveness that we will spend eternity with Him in Heaven.

In Matthew chapter 28, Jesus tells us to go out into all the world and preach the Gospel. He does not tell us, "Stay where you are comfortable, whisper my wonders, and hope that people will hear you." We are to tell anyone and everyone and shout it from the rooftops! This includes our neighbors, the people at work we do not really care for, and even the random people we encounter at the store or on the street. We are not to be shy about our faith. If other people had been quiet about theirs and kept it to themselves, would you have heard of the love of Christ and joined His family? Maybe, but it may have been years later, and you may have gone down a terrible path of life before coming to Christ. You could have missed out on so many years of building a relationship with God and experiencing His love.

We do not know when our last breath will be, so live your life like today is your last. Share the many wonderful things that God has done in your life, and tell everyone you know. Show people the love that He has shown you, even the people you do not like, and even in a hard situation when someone hurts you. This is what Jesus did and what God tells us to do. In 1 John 4:19-20, it says, **"We love because he [God] first loved us. If anyone says, 'I love God,' and hates his brother, he is a liar."** If we say we love God, this insinuates we love all people. So, if we say we love God but treat others terribly, we do not really love them, which means we have broken God's commandment. If people see us acting this way, they will feel hurt and sometimes just write off Christians altogether, which means we are not reaching the world as we have been commanded. We want to love people, to care for them, and to show them how much Jesus wants them to be a part of His family. In order to reach these people, we have to become uncomfortable.

I GOT IT
DEVOTION #5 - KARSEN THEEDE

"If you want something done right, do it yourself." This saying is the perfect representation of independence, something we all strive for in some fashion in our lives. We teach kids how to use the toilet on their own, brush their teeth, and dress themselves so that it is ingrained in them. When those kids get older, we teach them how to drive so they can get themselves places. Eventually, these kids grow up and reach a final state of independence when they move out and live on their own. Everyone is taught independence from a young age, though some like independence more than others. The "do it yourself" or "DIY" mentality is another example where instead of hiring a professional, even though sometimes you should, you decide that you have everything under control and you can handle it. We all feel the need to be independent, but there are some things in life that we cannot do on our own. Luckily, God has not asked us to. Instead, He provided a way for us, so are you ready to surrender that independence and discover His plans for you?

Presently, we are in our Reach, Gather, Grow series, where we are taking a look at the book of Ephesians. This week, we are focusing specifically on Reach in chapter 2. Ephesians 2:1-3 says, **"And you were dead in the trespasses and sins in which you once walked, following the course of this world, following the prince of the power of the air, the spirit that is now at work in the sons of disobedience - among whom we all once lived in the passions of our flesh, carrying out the desires of the body and the mind, and were by nature children of wrath, like the rest of mankind."**

Ephesians 2:8-9 adds, *"For by grace you have been saved through faith. And this is not your own doing; it is the gift of God, not a result of works, so that no one may boast."*

We can see in Ephesians that when we are independent from God, we walk in sin and live in our disobedience to God. We cannot save ourselves from our sins, but as we continue reading, we see that God has provided a way to salvation. That way is the gift of grace, not our works or independence, but our faith in God. God, thankfully, has not called us to save ourselves, but instead, to rely on His grace in sending His Son as a payment for our sins. By having faith in God and His sacrifice, we are saved from our sins and trespasses that we once walked in.

So, are you ready to sacrifice your independence? In exchange for our independence, we receive God's free gift of salvation. By accepting His salvation, we are no longer dead in our sins, but we are alive in Christ. We cannot rely on our works to save us, because, as Ephesians tells us, our salvation comes from God, so that no one may boast about their works, but only about God's free gift of grace.

BUT GOD
DEVOTION #6 - RICH SAWICKI

Although we are Christians, we are not perfect. Take a moment to think back to the exact moment you accepted Jesus as your Savior. It was the moment when you believed Jesus died for your sins and rose from the grave. This is when you accepted what God did. It is only because of what God did that we have grace through faith in Jesus.

Read this Scripture and reflect on your journey from death to life: ***"All of us also lived among them at one time, gratifying the cravings of our flesh and following its desires and thoughts. Like the rest, we were by nature deserving of wrath. But because of his great love for us, God, who is rich in mercy, made us alive with Christ even when we were dead in transgressions - it is by grace you have been saved"*** (Ephesians 2:3-5, NIV).

Think of a time when you felt you could not make it, and now, looking back, you realize you made it because God was with you. That is a "but God" moment.

Paul reminds us that we all come from the same place. We were all children of wrath. Wrath means great anger that desires to punish. Our sinful desires punish us by making us believe a perfect God would not love us. However, it is the "but God" mindset tells us that even before we were born, God chose us.

None of us got to pick our parents or where we were born, but God did. We grew up with choices made for us, but God was there. Now that we are grown, we have choices to make every day. Will we grow in His Word by reading or listening to the Bible? Will we follow what it says? Will we talk with God through prayer and listening? Will we give up the past for a better future?

These are questions we answer by how we live our lives. Yet remember, nothing can separate you from the love of Christ. Jesus loves you, no matter what.

I remember a time when I was overwhelmed with anxiety about my future. I felt stuck and hopeless, "but God" stepped in. Through a friend, I found a supportive community that counseled me. I felt God's peace and guidance, transforming my despair into hope. That moment reminded me of His constant love and mercy.

Think about your "but God" moment. How has understanding God's mercy and grace changed your life? How can you live out this truth every day?

Prayer: Lord, thank You for Your great love and mercy. Thank You for making us alive with Christ. Help us live each day in gratitude and show Your love to others. May we always remember the power of "but God." Amen.

LESSON TWO

GATHER

PASTOR PHILIP PIASECKI

When I was growing up, my family and I attended The River Church, Waterford location. I was there from the age of 5 to the age of 22, when I left with my wife to become the Worship Director at what is now The River Church, Grand Blanc location. When the Lord brought us back to the Waterford location in 2020, it felt like a blast from the past. I have distinct memories of being in late elementary school and early middle school, singing on the stage in the Waterford auditorium to a track on tape at our Saturday night gatherings. I would be a rich man if I had a dollar for every time I sang *"I Can Only Imagine."* I remember being so awkward and probably not the best singer, but it is still where my love for worship music really started to grow. Now, here I am in my mid-30s, leading from that same stage, trying to help us all understand just what this whole "gathering" thing really is and why it always seems to involve singing.

1. When you were in school, were you ever involved in singing at church, school talent shows, or plays? What is your best memory from those things?

_____
_____
_____

When the Church gathers together, there are certain activities that go together like little Lego bricks to complete what we call a "gathering." Normally, we always have the preaching of God's Word, prayer, musical worship, and some form of offering. Periodically, we will take communion, have baptisms, dedicate children, and that list could go on and on. I think the idea of preaching being a part of a church gathering makes sense to everyone. I have never heard anyone ask, "Do we have to have a sermon today?" However, what I have heard is that people question why we sing at our gatherings. We are going to look at a few different reasons in Scripture why we are commanded to sing in worship to the Lord. When writing to the Church in Ephesians 5:18-21, Paul says, **"And do not get drunk with wine, for that is debauchery, but be filled with the Spirit, addressing one another in psalms and hymns and spiritual songs, singing and making melody to the Lord with your heart,** *giving thanks always and for everything to God the Father in the name of our Lord Jesus Christ, submitting to one another out of reverence for Christ."*

2. Have you ever questioned why we sing in gatherings?
___
___
___

3. How are we commanded to sing in this Scripture?
___
___
___

First, it is simply because God has commanded us to do so. I know nobody likes to hear the answer, "Because I said so." We are going to look at the reasons why God commands us to sing, but first, we have to trust that when God tells us to do something in Scripture, it is ultimately for His glory and for our good. According to the book *"Sing"* by Keith and Kristyn Getty, the word sing appears in the Scriptures over 400 times, and at least 50 are commands. As Paul addresses the Ephesian church, he tells them to sing and make a melody to the Lord. Our praise comes out of the overflow of our thankful hearts for what Jesus has done for us. It is assumed in Scripture that when we really understand what Christ has done for us, what He has truly saved us from, that we will not even be able to contain our worship of Him.

Psalm 145:2-3 says, *"Every day I will bless you and praise your name forever and ever. Great is the Lord, and greatly to be praised, and his greatness is unsearchable."*

4. Do you find yourself often in awe of God and who He is?
___
___
___

5. If you believe this Scripture to be true, that He is **"greatly to be praised,"** What stops you from praising Him?

_____

_____

_____

Looking back at Ephesians 5:18-21, we see that we are commanded not only to make a melody to the Lord, but to actually address one another in psalms, hymns, and spiritual songs. When we sing, we actually encourage those who are around us. We are singing the truths of Scripture together and collectively being reminded about who God really is. One people with one voice lifting up a song to Jesus strengthens each person in that room. As you sang about God being faithful, someone in that room needed to be reminded of that, and you contributed to encouraging them! This Scripture should encourage us to actively engage in our gatherings. Gatherings are not a spectator sport. I promise you there are much better singers and bands you can go sit and listen to; what we do is collectively come together to worship at the feet of Jesus and to be encouraged by one another through those words.

6. How has the singing of other people in a gathering encouraged or impacted you?

_____

_____

_____

Matthew 26:30-32 records, **"And when they had sung a hymn, they went out to the Mount of Olives. Then Jesus said to them, 'You will all fall away because of me this night. For it is written, 'I will strike the shepherd, and the sheep of the flock will be scattered.' But after I am raised up, I will go before you to Galilee.'"**

7. Why do you think Scripture mentions that the disciples and Jesus sang together?

_____

_____

_____

Worshiping God through song prepares our hearts for what God is going to do. Here in Matthew, Jesus and the disciples sang a hymn of worship to God before heading out to the Mount of Olives, where Jesus would warn them about what was about to happen with His crucifixion. When we worship through song during a gathering, the Holy Spirit is working on our hearts, preparing us to hear from the Lord through the songs and the preaching. As worship leaders, we understand that each person brings in their own baggage from the week or even from that morning, and the whole world competes for our attention. It is easy to come to gatherings distracted, so we worship through singing to bring the attention of our hearts and minds toward Christ. My hope each Sunday is that even if you do not feel like you want to sing at the beginning of the gathering, by the end of the gathering, you are thankful that you submitted to the Lord's commands and worshiped Him even when you may not have felt like it.

8. How have you experienced Christ use corporate worship through singing to change your heart?

_____

_____

_____

In Acts 16:25-26, we read, *"About midnight Paul and Silas were praying and singing hymns to God, and the prisoners were listening to them, and suddenly there was a great earthquake, so that the foundations of the prison were shaken. And immediately all the doors were opened, and everyone's bonds were unfastened."*

9. Why do you think singing in worship can have such an effect on our attitude and perspective?

_____
_____
_____

10. Why do you think Paul and Silas were singing hymns to God while in jail?

_____
_____
_____

Maybe Paul and Silas were singing praise to the Lord because they knew the Scriptures that tell us to praise God in the good times and the hard times. They could have been singing because they needed to be reminded of the truths of God that they were struggling with at the time. I know that through their worship, God prepared their hearts for what was going to happen next, and He performed a miracle to release them from prison and save the soul of the jailer. I want to warn all of us as well that a hard and bitter heart will reject worshiping the Lord through singing. Paul and Silas could have been angry with the Lord for their circumstance; instead, they worshiped Him! If you find yourself more focused on critiquing the songs, the gathering, the ability of the band, or the hundreds of other things we can find to be critical about, I would ask you to search the condition of your heart. If your life is rooted in Christ and filled with the Spirit of God, then your heart should desire to worship the Lord by singing His praises. Let us lift up a joyful noise to the Lord together each and every time we gather together.

"Oh sing to the LORD a new song; sing to the LORD, all the earth! Sing to the LORD, bless his name; tell of his salvation from day to day." Psalm 96:1-2

"Praise the Lord! Praise God in his sanctuary; praise him in his mighty heavens! Praise him for his mighty deeds; praise him according to his excellent greatness!" Psalm 150:1-2

NOTES

STANDING STRONG TOGETHER
DEVOTION #1 - MARK PITTENGER

As I have become more bold in representing Jesus, I have noticed that people will often ask similar questions when confronted with the Gospel. It is typically something like, "How do you know the Bible is true? Isn't the Bible just written by men?" The other day, I was having a conversation with a coworker who proclaims to be a Christian, and he said, "The Bible has great moral teachings but none of the stories can be factually proven." I was reminded of this conversation when I read Ephesians 4:11-14, which says, *"And he gave the apostles, the prophets, the evangelists, the shepherds and teachers, to equip the saints for the work of ministry, for building up the body of Christ, until we all attain to the unity of the faith and of the knowledge of the Son of God, to mature manhood, to the measure of the stature of the fullness of Christ, so that we may no longer be children, tossed to and fro by the waves and carried about by every wind of doctrine, by human cunning, by craftiness in deceitful schemes."*

Paul is saying that, within the Church, God has given different abilities to different people so that we need each other. The entire design of the Church is one body with many members and each member plays a vital role. Some are given the ability to teach others the truth of the Gospel, and it is only when we can get on one accord with that truth that we can grow together as the Church.

As with the story of my coworker, as well as many others, they are not fully grounded in the truth of the Gospel of Jesus. This gives way for these false teachings to persuade them into questioning the very truth of God's Word. This is what Paul is referring to when he says,

"That we may no longer be children, tossed to and fro by the waves and carried about by every wind of doctrine, by human cunning, by craftiness in deceitful schemes."

The phrases **"wind of doctrine," "human cunning,"** and **"craftiness in deceitful schemes"** are great examples of the enemy's only means of battling God: confusion. As he did in the garden with Adam and Eve, and as he does to this very day, the devil creates confusion by saying, "Did God really say that?" When we gather together and grow together as the Church, we become more and more confident in the truth of God's Word, in the truth of the Gospel, and in our walk with Jesus. Things that were once unclear, become as crystals, and we become more bold in our faith. This is why gathering together with other Bible-believing saints is an important and necessary piece of our ever-growing walk with Jesus.

Proverbs 27:17 adds, **"Iron sharpens iron, and one man sharpens another."**

PARTICIPATION AWARD
DEVOTION #2 - MELVIN FRICK

"Addressing one another in psalms and hymns and spiritual songs, singing and making melody to the Lord with your heart." Ephesians 5:19

Most believers will agree that gathering as the church should include fellowship. I could not think of a better verse in the Bible to illustrates what fellowship ought to look like other than Ephesians 5:19. Does it have to include addressing one another specifically in psalms, hymns, and spiritual songs? Of course not. The Bible says, **"Whatever you do, in word or deed, do everything in the name of the Lord Jesus, giving thanks to God the Father through him"** (Colossians 3:17). By no means would it be wrong to address one another in this way, but I believe the lesson we should learn from this text is to be intentional about fellowship when we gather. We need to be doing it all in the name of our Lord Jesus, giving thanks to God through Him for the wonderful blessing we have, including one another.

So, what does the word fellowship really mean? In the original language, this word (κοινωνία or koinonia) means participation. This is a critical part of the gathering as the church. We should not only be willing to genuinely connect with others, but actively participating in the life of the church and in the lives of the believers God has placed around us.

With this in mind, I would like to ask the question, "Would you rather receive a first-place trophy or a participation award?" The answer is simple for me – a first-place trophy, ten out of ten times. However, when I stop to think about why that is, the answer is clear: I like it when people are proud of me. I like when the hard work I put into something is noticed. There is nothing wrong with this, yet the church is the only place where receiving the participation award is greater than receiving the first-place trophy. More importantly, Christ is most proud when we are actively participating in each other's lives, in a manner of love for His name's sake.

May we keep the word "participation" at the forefront of our minds as we gather together as the church and remember in our hearts which award Christ desires to confer upon His beloved.

GATHERING AS THE CHURCH
DEVOTION #3 - CAMERON ALDRICH

In the mid-1800s, Abner Doubleday introduced a game that required players to not only have talent, but also have the ability to work as part of a team to be successful. The game of baseball has been our nation's favorite pastime ever since. Do you think any team has ever won a game without having an essential position playing on the field? Every position in baseball is important and has its role, and no team can find success without having each of them.

Even though the church is not the same as your favorite baseball team, the church can still be thought of as a team. There are many different positions that make up the body of Christ. Each position holds an indispensable value in growing the Kingdom and sharing the Gospel of Jesus.

In Ephesians chapter 4, Paul shares that when Christ ascended on high, He gave gifts to men. In verses 11-12, he expresses that Christ **"gave the apostles, the prophets, the evangelists, the shepherds and teachers, to equip the saints for the work of ministry, for building up the body of Christ."** In verse 13, Paul shares that our goal in working as the body of Christ remains **"until we all attain to the unity of the faith and of the knowledge of the Son of God."** We can strive to achieve this goal when we, as followers of Christ, remain faithful and diligent in our role as part of the body of Christ regardless of what specific position we fill, no matter if we are a leader in the church or a volunteer behind the scenes.

There is an incredibly important action that we should all consistently cling to which will further help us achieve the goal that Paul shares to us in Ephesians: gathering as the church.

Being together, whether in the larger context of a Sunday gathering or in a smaller context such as a Growth Community, is so much more than just going through the motions of a typical Christian routine. When we are separated, we become weak, our strength falters, and we are vulnerable to failure. God did not intend for us to be alone in our walk of faith. It is crucial that we gather together as the body.

Later in Ephesians chapter 4, Paul shares why our goal is to be unified in our faith and knowledge of Christ as believers. In verse 14, he expresses that this is **"so that we may no longer be children, tossed to and fro by the waves and carried about by every wind of doctrine, by human cunning, by craftiness in deceitful schemes."** We can relate Paul's mentioning of being children to being young and immature in our faith as believers.

An important responsibility of being on a baseball team is that you as a player have to hold yourself accountable by understanding what your weaknesses are and how those can affect the team's success. Another major responsibility is that, in knowing your flaws as a player, you will also be diligent in strengthening those flaws with a desire to become better.

As a part of the body of Christ, we have the exact same responsibility. Christ has given us all that we need to carry out the work of ministry, and one invaluable weapon that we have at our disposal is the ability to gather as the church. When we gather, our focus is reset, our minds are sharpened, our hearts are softened, and our spiritual strength is renewed.

The church has the opportunity to gather on a consistent basis. We must not fail to take advantage of that fact. It is our responsibility as a follower of Christ. When we are unified and together as a body, we are strong.

MAKE A JOYFUL NOISE!
DEVOTION #4 - SIERRA COMBS

I recently got back from an amazing trip overseas. We had the whole thing extensively planned and packed with sightseeing, not wanting to miss a single thing. We woke up early every morning and stayed out late every night. We were happy but exhausted. It was not until about halfway through the trip that we finally had a morning to sleep in. I went to bed, savoring the fact that I could wake up without an alarm, and even took my time going to bed because of it. This was a mistake. At around 6:30 a.m., the noise started. At first, it sounded like a man with an instrument and a loudspeaker. I tuned it out and went back to sleep. Soon after, other instruments joined, and I was absolutely confused as to why a concert was happening outside of our hotel at seven in the morning (on a Wednesday). By 7:15, a bunch of people had gathered with drums and horns and decided it was time to make the most insufferable sound that quite possibly has ever existed, over and over and over again. Think of the loudest, most annoying alarm noise on your iPhone and multiply the volume level by 100. Add a couple of bullhorns, a kick drum, and the screams and shouts of dozens of people protesting plastic, and you can imagine my horror. It was the most terrible noise I have ever heard. By this time, there was absolutely no option to go back to sleep, so I ventured out to get some coffee, passing the scene and stopping to talk to some police who agreed that while it was absolutely ridiculous, they still had the right to protest and make that terrible noise. As angry as I was at the time, I will give them this: these people sure knew how to come together in like-mindedness, passionately raising their voices for all to hear. They did not care about what anyone thought, what they sounded like, or how they looked. They just wanted to proclaim their message for everyone around to hear.

As silly as it is, this reminds me of another group of people who have been commanded to come together and make noise, and not just a loud noise, but a joyful noise unto the Lord! Psalm 95:2 tells us, **"Come into His presence with thanksgiving; let us make a joyful noise to Him with songs of praise!"** Psalm 98:4-9 commands us, **"Make a joyful noise to the Lord, all the earth; break forth into joyous song and sing praises! Sing praises to the Lord with the lyre, with the lyre and the sound of melody! With trumpets and the sound of the horn make a joyful noise before the King, the Lord! Let the sea roar, and all that fills it; the world and those who dwell in it! Let the rivers clap their hands; let the hills sing for joy together before the Lord."**

Just picture it: all of God's creations are passionately coming together to worship Him! This is what we are called to do. While every day is a day to praise and worship the Lord in our own personal way, He has instructed us to gather together with our brothers and sisters in Christ on a regular basis and make that joyful noise. Ephesians 5:18-21 tells us, **"Be filled with the Spirit, addressing one another in psalms and hymns and spiritual songs, singing and making melody to the Lord with your heart, giving thanks always and for everything to God the Father in the name of our Lord Jesus Christ, submitting to one another out of reverence for Christ."** We should find so much joy in the Lord that we cannot help but express it. It should just pour out of us! The next time you gather on a Sunday, I encourage you to think upon all of the good things the Lord has done and is doing and let thankfulness and joy overflow as you worship Him. Set aside self-consciousness and worries about what others are thinking. Proclaim God's goodness for everyone to hear and make a joyful noise!

UNITY
DEVOTION #5 - DEBBIE GABBARA

"And he gave the apostles, the prophets, the evangelists, the shepherds and teachers, to equip the saints for the work of ministry, for building up the body of Christ, until we all attain to the unity of the faith and of the knowledge of the Son of God, to mature manhood, to the measure of the stature of the fullness of Christ, so that we may no longer be children, tossed to and fro by the waves and carried about by every wind of doctrine, by human cunning, by craftiness in deceitful schemes." Ephesians 4:11-14

Unity: the state of being united or joined as a whole.

We have all been part of a group or team at one time or another. It could be sports teams, work teams, musical groups, dance groups, or even teams in a game. No matter what kind of group or team we are a part of, it is crucial that we work together to achieve the goal.

A dancer turning to the right when everyone else goes left would throw off all the other dancers. Imagine if a baseball player hit the ball and then ran to third base instead of first; that would certainly create confusion among the players. If all the individuals in a symphony played at the tempo they decided sounded best, it would be painful to listen to. However, sports teams have coaches, dancers have instructors, and in a symphony, there is a conductor who unifies the musicians and guides the orchestra to create beautiful music and bring his vision to life.

Unity is a common topic in the Bible. The Bible calls the entirety of the body of believers the Church. Throughout Scripture we see the Lord teaching us to work together, to worship Him, and to lead others to find faith in the One True God.

The body of believers here at The River Church has teams that serve in many capacities. There are opportunities to serve and grow in the Lord in all areas of the ministry. God calls pastors and teachers to encourage and train us. Here in Ephesians, Paul reminds us that every believer is meant to grow in spiritual maturity and to share our love for God and for others. Together, we, the church, gather to grow in knowledge by studying God's Word, which will help us become rooted and mature in our faith in Christ Jesus.

God, our conductor, has a plan for every believer. He wants to use each one of us to spread the incredible news of salvation through Christ Jesus. As we love God and others, we find joy in gathering and worshiping Him together in this beautiful symphony called life.

Philippians 2:1-2 says, **"So if there is any encouragement in Christ, any comfort from love, any participation in the Spirit, any affection and sympathy, complete my joy by being of the same mind, having the same love, being in full accord and of one mind."**

EVERYONE IS NEEDED
DEVOTION #6 - DR. RANDY T. JOHNSON

"And he gave the apostles, the prophets, the evangelists, the shepherds and teachers, to equip the saints for the work of ministry, for building up the body of Christ, until we all attain to the unity of the faith and of the knowledge of the Son of God, to mature manhood, to the measure of the stature of the fullness of Christ." Ephesians 4:11-13

When I was in college, I had a beautiful Honda Cb750 motorcycle. It was a deep red/maroon with some black and gold trim. The windshield (fairing) continued the design. It even had matching helmets. The seat was custom and comfortable, enclosed by a padded "sissy bar." It was sweet, or "fly," as we used to say.

One afternoon, when I was riding home, I had a learning experience that taught me so much more. I was driving on the south side of Eight Mile Road, and my bike just died. I pushed it off to the side of the road and released the gas cap. There was plenty of fuel. This was the 80s, so I did not have a cell phone. There was no way I was going to just leave it as I walked home or looked for a phone booth. I had to start pushing my 500-pound baby. Several drivers slowed up, rolled down their windows, and asked if I had run out of gas. I replied, "No."

Finally, one guy pulled over and came out of his car. After asking about the fuel, he popped off the side panel of my prized possession. He pointed out it had blown a fuse. Fortunately, there was a spare fuse fastened to the panel. He plugged it in and my ride purred beautifully. He encouraged to make sure I replaced the spare fuse.

I did. It cost me a quarter. It is amazing that a 25 cent piece could shut down everything.

I find this to be such an accurate picture of the church. Everyone is needed.

- It does not matter if your position is visible to all.
- It does not matter if you are not flashy (a lot of parts of my bike were dipped in chrome and had a special shine to them).
- It does not matter if you are thought of as replaceable, insignificant, unimportant, or just a 25 cent piece.

Every part and everyone is needed. God has placed **"apostles, the prophets, the evangelists, the shepherds and teachers, to equip the saints."** However, the church needs **"saints"** who serve in the nursery, greet people at the door, make coffee, pray for the gatherings, help in the kids' ministry, host a Growth Community, encourage others, monitor the sound, serve as gathering hosts, prepare communion, make sure everyone is safe, lead worship, wash dishes, help with student ministry, pull weeds, organize craft material, clean bathrooms, drive a bus, make hospital visits, set up chairs, answer phones, distribute food, register kids, run a camera, maintain vehicles, provide information at guest services, prepare snacks, and help growth become contagious. Remember, a missing or faulty part can disrupt the whole machine. I may not be able to do everything, but I can do something.

LESSON THREE

GROW

PASTOR ROY TOWNSEND

It is amazing how quickly we can run from one thing to another. When I became a teacher and then later a father, it would astonish me how quickly children can run from one thing to the next. It can almost be overwhelming.

1. Please describe a time when you or your family had a really hard time staying focused on the task at hand.

_____
_____
_____

If we are being honest, it is really hard to concentrate sometimes. Even when it comes to our spiritual walk, God's children can jump from one spiritually-sounding topic to the next. What seems to happen is that this process can often confuse others. Henry Ironside wrote, "Very often when one is trying to open up some line of truth to believers, he is embarrassed by the questions that are asked showing that there is no concentration, no follow up of the truth already before them, and as a result people are never truly established."

2. What is a current topic within the Church that is causing God's children to be confused? Do you feel overwhelmed?

_____
_____
_____

In the book of Ephesians, we are warned about this. Ephesians 4:14 reads, **"So that we may no longer be children, tossed to and fro by the waves and carried about by every wind of doctrine, by human cunning, by craftiness in deceitful schemes."** The warning with this verse relays that we are to "grow-up," and not be like children because children jump back and forth or are **"tossed to and fro."** I just really like using the word **"fro."** Moreover, this verse speaks directly to our topic of being carried around by all these new doctrines. I love how the Scripture gives us a picture of being caught in the surf of the ocean as the waves crash into the shore. I have been there, and I have been stuck there before, too. It was really hard to get out of the water.

3. Have you or your family ever been caught up in a doctrine that proved to be false? Please share with the group, and explain how you got out of this situation.

_____
_____
_____

4. Would you define this false doctrine as **"by human cunning, by craftiness in deceitful schemes"**? Why?

_____
_____
_____

Well, if we go back a few verses to verse 12, it explains how we can keep from being distracted or chasing after the "next best thing" spiritually. Ephesians 4:12-13 reads, **"To equip the saints for the work of ministry, for building up the body of Christ, until we all attain to the unity of the faith and of the knowledge of the Son of God, to mature manhood, to the measure of the stature of the fullness of Christ."** So, the goal here is for the Church to be equipped.

5. Before we discuss being equipped, how have you been equipped for the work of the ministry? Please explain.

_____
_____
_____

6. Or, how have you not been equipped for the work of the ministry? Please explain.

_____
_____
_____

As I studied for this lesson, the Apostle Paul used an interesting word that we translated as equipped. William Barclay writes, "The word is used in surgery for setting a broken limb or for putting a joint back into its place. In politics it is used for bringing together opposing factions so that the government can go on...The basic idea of the word is that of putting a thing into the condition in which it ought to be." So, this would lead us to believe, as the Scripture noted, that we ought to **"attain to the unity of the faith and of the knowledge of the Son of God, to mature manhood, to the measure of the stature of the fullness of Christ."** Rather, this should be done when the leadership of the Church takes seriously the fact that God has given gifted leadership to the Church, and He has given His Word to the saints so that we can submit to this equipping of the saints.

7. What has been most helpful to your spiritual growth as you have been equipped for the work of the ministry?

_____
_____
_____

8. How should this be done? Is it just the job of the pastors or staff to equip the saints?

_____
_____
_____

Lastly, we read in Ephesians 4:15-16, **"Rather, speaking the truth in love, we are to grow up in every way into him who is the head, into Christ, from whom the whole body, joined and held together by every joint with which it is equipped, when each part is working properly, makes the body grow so that it builds itself up in love."** We get to the beautiful ending of this section of Scripture. We must speak the truth and the great truth revealed by God to us. Henry Ironside wrote, "It is God's own blessed Word, and you can depend upon it. You can live upon it, and as you feed upon the precious truth here revealed, you will grow in grace and in the knowledge of our Lord and Savior, Jesus Christ."

9. When reading Ephesians 4:15-16, there is a direction and a warning. Why do you think the Scripture is translated as **"speaking the truth in love"**? What is the truth/warning?

_____
_____
_____

I often see two problems. We either have many who are not really equipped for the work because there is no foundation built upon God's Word, or those who have a firm foundation of the knowledge of God's Word but no focus on His love for us and others or our love of God and others. We must not forget the great fundamental truth is love. In 1 Corinthians 13:2-3, we read, **"And if I have prophetic powers, and understand all mysteries and all knowledge, and if I have all faith, so as to remove mountains, but have not love, I am nothing. If I give away all I have, and if I deliver up my body to be burned, but have not love, I gain nothing."**

10. Do you struggle with the truth, or do you struggle with love? Explain.

_____
_____
_____

NOTES

TALK THE TALK
DEVOTION #1 - GRANT GRIMES

"Let no corrupting talk come out of your mouths, but only such as is good for building up, as fits the occasion, that it may give grace to those who hear." Ephesians 4:29

There is a popular phrase we often hear about speech or talking: "If you are going to talk the talk, then you better walk the walk." I want to bring up this phrase because we often, as Christians, neglect to control our speech. So often in our lives, we choose to follow Christ, yet our everyday speech and tone do not follow our new direction. We continue to cuss, speak in harmful ways, cut people down, and truly dishonor God with our words. Our words are, as Paul says, corrupt, or a better term in my opinion, rotten. Our speech is putrid and forces people to walk away with not only a bad sense of us, but of the One our life is supposed to be pointed.

If our speech is supposed to be without corruption, then what is our speech supposed to look like? This is the aspect where growth mindset comes into play. Once you have accepted Christ as your Savior, you are to grow in relation to and emulate Christ. A great reminder for me is found in 1 Corinthians 6:20, *"For you were bought with a price. So glorify God in your body."* We were bought with a price so we must honor God with every aspect of who we are, including our speech. If we are going to walk with the Lord and grow in our relationship, we have to "talk the talk" as well. I love when Paul talks about *"building up."* When I was studying this part of the passage, I saw an interpretation of bringing something closer to completion or fullness. That is what our speech should do: bring people closer to completeness, which is Jesus Christ, the founder and perfecter of our faith.

In breaking down the next portion of this verse, I think the best translation comes from the New Living Translation, which says, **"according to their needs."** Our speech is supposed to help the needs of the people around us. As a Christian, a part of growing in Christ is living a life of servitude. I really think this relates to our speech as well. If people leave our conversations with rudeness, hurt, and pain, are we truly serving the Lord with our speech? Does our speech build up and serve the needs that are around us?

Paul finishes with the theme of grace. Do our words lead people back to the grace of God? Jesus Christ has died for all sin and extended grace upon grace. Do we live a life in which our conversations point toward Christ? If they do not, then that is where we need to grow, speak words that raise people up, fit their needs, and show the love of Christ.

WORDS ARE HARD!
DEVOTION #2 - JOSH THAYER

I am not one of those people who feels the weight of words. Most of the time, I cannot even remember the conversation I had just five minutes ago. (That is the opposite of my wife. She can remember word for word, a conversation we had five years ago. It is a superpower.) It takes effort for me to slow down and really think my words through. Here in Ephesians, Paul is saying that words actually do matter in every circumstance, and we need to be mindful of them.

Ephesians 4:29 says, **"Let no corrupting talk come out of your mouths, but only such as is good for building up, as fits the occasion, that it may give grace to those who hear."**

Paul is getting real with us here about the power of our words. He is essentially saying, "Hey, watch what comes out of your mouth!" You know what? He is onto something big here.

Think about it. How often do we let negative, hurtful, or just plain old gossip-filled words slip out? It is so easy to get caught up in complaining, criticizing, or tearing others down. However, Paul is reminding us that our words have consequences. They have power to either teardown or to build up.

So, what kind of talk should be coming out of our mouths? Paul has clear instruction for us. He says our talk should be good for building others up! Our words should be like little bricks, stacking up to create something strong and beautiful - not ripping down what has already been built.

Here is the kicker: our words should fit the occasion. We need to be mindful of the situation we are in and the people we are talking to. Sometimes, a joke just might lighten the mood, but other times, a word of encouragement or a listening ear might be needed most.

Here is the best part: when we use our words to build up others (when we speak words of grace and kindness), it is not just good for them; it is good for us, too! Paul says our words should **"give grace to those who hear."** That means when we speak life-giving words, we are spreading grace and showing others God's love and goodness.

As we go about our day today, let us remember the power of our words. Let us choose to speak words that build up, encourage, and spread grace like wildfire. When we do this, we are not just making the world a better place for others, but we are living out the love of Christ in a tangible way. That, my friends, is something worth talking about.

GROWING IN DIFFICULTY
DEVOTION #3 - ALYSSA FAIRSE

I came to know Jesus as my Savior when I was 14 years old. I was in the foster care system. I had just gone back to Children's Village for a second time in their shelter building because I had no family and no home. I hear it often, "So many people in your situation would have turned to drugs, sex, alcohol, or whatever." Truth be told, I would have if Jesus did not meet me exactly where I was. There I was, alone. My mother was a drug addict. My father was nowhere to be found. My brother wanted nothing to do with me and he was being adopted by a family who wanted nothing to do with me. Lastly, there was my grandfather, the one who abused me, the one I blamed for putting me here. I thought, "How is it that I have spent my entire childhood being abused by this man, and yet I am the one locked up here?" I was furious. Little did I know God was saving me from myself by putting me in a place where I was free to grow in Him.

I spent my first month there weeping every day. I was feeling sorry for myself, that no one loved me or wanted me. In my second month, I met Mrs. Goforth. She gave me a Bible, she prayed with me, and she told me about the everlasting love of Jesus. Jesus intervened. He met me exactly where I was, and I gave my life to Him. I spent my third month there praying, learning about Jesus, and learning to forgive my biological family for all they had done. I can confidently say I left Children's Village a completely different person than I was when I first walked in.

It is only through the divine power of Jesus Christ that I am where I am today. I could not have pulled myself out of that situation and become the person I am today on my own. It is only because I belong to Christ that I have any wisdom and am of any sound mind at all.

Ephesians 2:8 says, ***"For by grace you have been saved through faith. And this is not your own doing; it is the gift of God."***

It is easy to be complacent, to be idle, and to stay the same. I know first-hand just how hard this life can get and how easy it is to stay in the same place, especially when we are trapped in our emotions of feeling sorry for ourselves. Ultimately, because change is hard. It is uncomfortable to know that we are not the same person we were a year ago, six months ago, or even a week ago. God has called us to do more. He has called us to grow. We are imperfect, and because of that, we have a never-ending need to change. God is the only one who is never changing, the only one who is consistently who He says He is (Hebrews 13:8), and because of that, we will always have a never-ending need for God. God is where we should get our wisdom, knowledge, love for others, and forgiveness for others. Otherwise, we are not growing, we are just filling our minds with ourselves. That is full of flesh and sin (Ephesians 2:1-3).

Today, I encourage you to allow God to intervene in your life. Whatever you are going through, whether it is a difficult season or a season of complacency, be so obedient to the Word of God that you have no other choice but to grow in Jesus.

IMITATORS OF CHRIST
DEVOTION #4 - PASTOR MITCHELL HOLMES

They say that imitation is the sincerest form of flattery, and I think I began to appreciate that phrase more fully when I started dating my wife. When I first met her, her vocabulary (as well as mine) was a lot different than it is today. As we spent more and more time together, we began to mimic one another in our mannerisms and phrases that we commonly said. There came a day when I realized that my wife had used a phrase three or four times in the span of a few hours that I had never heard her using just a few months prior. I felt an immense amount of pride and love when I realized that the phrase that she was using was one that she had picked up from me. I was proud that she thought I was hilarious enough to copy, but I also felt loved because she listened to the way I talked intently enough that it showed subconsciously in her speech. Our passage today asks us to keep this idea of imitation in mind as we grow in our walk with the Lord.

Ephesians 4:15-16 says, ***"Rather, speaking the truth in love, we are to grow up in every way into him who is the head, into Christ, from whom the whole body, joined and held together by every joint with which it is equipped, when each part is working properly, makes the body grow so that it builds itself up in love."*** This verse calls for Christians to grow to be as much like Christ as we possibly can be. As a Christian or "mini-Christ," we are expected to be as close a representation of Him as we can be. We are called to be ambassadors for Him in a broken and dark world in need of a Savior. We are, of course, flawed and sinful people who can never hope to match a fragment of the majesty and holiness of

God, but we are expected to continuously grow in every way to be as Christ-like as possible.

This is a very popular verse, and for good reason. We all struggle with the task of representing Christ well. For some of us, in an attempt to lead people to the grace and forgiveness found in Jesus, we will communicate the truth of God's Word but do so in a brute-force fashion. Here, in this passage, Paul is calling us to communicate the truth of God in love instead. Make sure that you speak with a gentle demeanor and show the person who you are speaking with that you are a safe person to talk to. Of course, we are supposed to aid people in repenting and believing in Christ. Since we love the people close to us, that means that we must speak the truth to them. Since we know the truth, love has to be what is most prominent in us, even when we call someone to cut out the sinful things in their lives.

Christ had an offensive message in His day, and of course, that did not stop Him from speaking truth to people, but He always did so with a tenderheartedness that characterized God's love. The best way that you can imitate Christ and show your love for Him and others is by loving them enough to tell them the truth with a careful gentleness that will demonstrate the love of Jesus to them.

PRAYING FOR GROWTH
DEVOTION #5 - LORENA HABER

In the first 14 verses of Ephesians, Paul describes spiritual blessings in Jesus. He praises God for His faithful character in compassion, forgiveness, grace, and the gift of the Holy Spirit. Then, in verses 15-17, Paul has heard the Ephesians' faith and their commitment to acting in love.

Ephesians 1:15-17 says, ***"For this reason, because I have heard of your faith in the Lord Jesus and your love toward all the saints, I do not cease to give thanks for you, remembering you in my prayers, that the God of our Lord Jesus Christ, the Father of glory, may give you the Spirit of wisdom and revelation in the knowledge of him."***

You can imagine the Church of Ephesus is in a fruitful season. They thrived on the spiritual blessings explained in the earlier verses. The word traveled so much that their reputation was becoming known. Paul appreciates and praises all the good things in the Church of Ephesus. Then, upon hearing these reports, Paul takes action. He begins to give thanks and remembers the Ephesians in his prayers. Paul prays for ***"the Spirit of wisdom and revelation in the knowledge of him."*** Paul is praying that this lively Church would continue to pursue holy and righteous things, which is the character of God! He is praying that the Church will continue to know Christ more.

What a profound prayer in such few words and such great circumstances. However, this prayer can feel unnatural to us. Why would a thriving church under such spiritual blessings need prayer? We naturally pray for circumstances to change when we see the world is fallen in nature. We often treat prayer as a crisis response. Yet, Paul flips this idea on its head. Paul does not pray for circumstances to change, but for the Church to seize opportunities to grow closer to God in wisdom and knowledge of Him. This prayer added fuel to a fire that is already burning for Christ. It reminds us that God is with us in times of great joy and great need. This prayer teaches us to pray for renewed strength, wisdom, growth, and dependency on Jesus instead of praying for the situation to change. Every moment, good or bad, is a moment for God's presence to invade and show us something new.

This does not dismiss prayers of lament, protest, healing, or deliverance. The Bible shows us many of these prayers and tells us to pray and care for those in need. Nevertheless, these verses show us how to pray for each other in all circumstances. When someone is down in a valley, they need your prayers. When someone is up on a mountain, they need your prayers. Who in your life is on a mountain? Who in your life is in a valley? Follow the example in Ephesians 1:15-17. Pray and give thanks to the Lord for that person in your life. Then, pray that God would give them wisdom. The goal is to receive that wisdom so that a person can grow in their relationship with their Creator.

WORDS MATTER
DEVOTION #6 - ZACH HONNEN

Growth looks different for every single one of us. No believer, no person is exactly alike. Each and every one of us has our own struggles, pitfalls, and besetting sins. However, each one of us is called to grow in our faith, in our relationship with Christ, and in our sanctification. Today, I want to hone in on what it looks like to grow and how we manage our mouths. To continue this study, let us look at our passage for today's devotional.

Ephesians 4:29 says, **"Let no corrupting talk come out of your mouths, but only such as is good for building up, as fits the occasion, that it may give grace to those who hear."**

We are all in a different place regarding how we talk. For example, I struggled with managing my language when I was younger, whereas my brother had no such issue. Yet, that is no excuse for any of us. Each one of us needs to learn to tame our tongue. **"Corrupting talk"** within the Greek refers to something that is foul, such as rotted fruit or putrid meat. Our words can bring life or the smell of death, depending on what we say and how we say things. If you have ever smelled rotten meat or had a rotten conversation, you know what this passage is talking about. For some of us, corrupt talk is using foul curse words. For some of us, it is the use of inappropriate jokes or comments. For others, it could even be gossip, but these things should not be on the lips of a Christian. It is not in Christ's character.

So, what then should be on our lips? Well, the apostle Paul says, **"Only such as is good for building up, as fits the occasion, that it may give grace to those who hear."**

As Christians, we are supposed to speak life and grace to one another and use words that fit the occasion. This passage does not tell us to be pushovers and never to speak, but it tells us that when we speak, it must be done as a Christian. It must be as if Christ is speaking. Jesus says, **"Blessed are the meek, for they shall inherit the earth"** (Matthew 5:5). This means power under control, which is what we are called to do. The tongue is mighty; it is like the rudder of a ship. It has the power to direct and lead people in different ways, and with that power must come great control. Self-control is a fruit of the Spirit, an area we all must grow in as we live out our Christian faith.

This week, I ask you to pray to God and ask Him to help tame your tongue. Spend time paying attention to what you say, reflecting on what you say, and either repenting or glorifying God for it. Out of the heart the mouth speaks (Luke 6:45), so, maybe it is time to ask God to clean out your heart and remember we are all at different places in our journey. For some of us, this is not a hard thing. For others, it is years of habits that we must overcome. So, remember to always have grace towards our brothers and sisters, and even non-believers, when it comes to the area of controlling the tongue.

LESSON FOUR

GIVING

PASTOR JOSH COMBS

I love the word "therefore" in the Bible. It tells us essentially, because of this, do that or do not do those things or think this way or do not think that way.

Towards the end of Ephesians chapter 4, we find a big **"therefore."** Paul is pivoting from the theological truths of the first few chapters to the issues of practical Christian living. He is going to talk about the nuts and bolts of Christianity or the "rubber meets the road stuff." Notice the order of the letter though: the foundation of theological truth, then practical living (not the other way around). Because of the profound mystery of Christ, because of the Gospel, because you have been made new, because you have been created (or recreated) in Christ Jesus…THEREFORE!

If that Gospel transformation has happened, here is what your transformed or renewed life will look like. The Apostle Paul seems to focus primarily on how our relationships will change. Marriage, parenting, co-workers, bosses, neighbors, and others are all addressed. Chapter 4 is a rapid-fire sequence of how Jesus transforms how we treat people.

4:25 - We do not lie, but we tell the truth.
4:26 - We get angry, but we do not hold a grudge.
4:28 - We do not steal, but work hard and share.
4:29 - We do not gossip, but we encourage.
4:30 - We are not bitter, resentful, or malicious, but tenderhearted and forgiving.

For this study guide, we are going to focus on one of these relationships.

Ephesians 4:28 says, **"Let the thief no longer steal, but rather let him labor, doing honest work with his own hands, so that he may have something to share with anyone in need."**

1. Have you ever been the victim of a thief? If so, what happened?

_____
_____
_____

There are whole industries that have been started to try to combat stealing. Think about the amount of scams and identify thefts that take place on a daily basis.

Stop and think: what have you done today (out of habit, without thinking about it) to combat somebody stealing from you? Can you list ten things?

1.
2.
3.
4.
5.
6.
7.
8.
9.
10.

Sadly, if we kept thinking about it, we could come up with dozens of things that we do, without even noticing, that are meant to keep us from being stolen from.

2. Tough question: have you ever stolen (took something that was not yours)? If so, what was the situation? (Avoid the "I stole a candy bar when I was a kid" stories. Be transparent.)

_____
_____
_____

The Good News of Jesus changes us. We have a *"such were some of you"* moment (Read 1 Corinthians 6:9-11). We are not thieves, swindlers, or con artists anymore. We have been made new.

In his letter to the Christians at Ephesus, Paul says, *"Did you use to make ends meet by stealing? Well, no more! Get an honest job so that you can help others who can't work."* (Ephesians 4:28, MSG)

We do not steal anymore; we work.

3. Read Ephesians 6:5-9 and Colossians 3:22-4:1. What does work look like for a Christian?

   _____
   _____
   _____

Christians should not steal. We should be the best employees and the best employers. That means we do not steal from our boss and we do not steal from our employees.

That seems basic; but why? Why should we be good workers? It is more than just to provide for our family. That is a good thing. See the progression of Ephesians 4:28. We do not steal from people anymore; we work *"so that [we]...have something to share with anyone in need."* Outside of Christ, our needs were more important than others. That is the mentality that leads to stealing, but it is also the attitude that leads to greed. If we just say, "Okay I will not steal anymore, I will earn what I have," we would still fall short of what Jesus wants for us. We work so we can give it away! Whoever said, "sharing is caring," was right.

4. How has someone shared with you at a moment when you were in need?

   _____
   _____
   _____

5. Have you ever thanked them? (If not, pause right now and text them, call them, or write them a thank you note.)

_____
_____
_____

6. Do you have somebody you need to share with? Who? How?

_____
_____
_____

7. How did the early church in Acts practice sharing? Read Acts 5:32-37.

_____
_____
_____

Because of what Christ has done, **"therefore,"** stop stealing, start working, and start sharing. Why? It is because of Christ's great gifts to us! He is the ultimate example of sharing.

8. What has Christ given to us?
    Ephesians 1:17 _____
    Ephesians 2:8 _____
    Ephesians 4:7 _____
    Ephesians 4:11-12 _____
    Ephesians 5:2, 25 _____

Our giving is a reflection of what Jesus Christ has given to us. How and how much we give is directly related to how we see the gift of God. When we are stingy, greedy, and selfish, we must return to the cross to see the greatest gift, given by the greatest giver and be inspired once again. That is the **"therefore"** moment we regularly need.

NOTES

"TO JOIN HIM IN HIS WORK"
DEVOTION #1 - PASTOR CHUCK LINDSEY

"Let him who stole steal no longer, but rather let him labor, working with his hands what is good, that he may have something to give him who has need." Ephesians 4:28 (NKJV)

One of the greatest joys we can experience in life is to join our Father in what He is doing.

It is like when a child "works" together with their father in the garage, shop, or mowing the lawn. The "help" certainly is not needed, but it is welcomed on both sides. The reason for this is simple: it is an expression of a relationship. A dad allows his child to help to be with his child in a special way. The child helps to be with their dad in a special way. Each benefits from the deepening of the relationship. This is what it is to be a follower of the Lord Jesus and give to those in need.

From a theological perspective, it is true that the Lord is limitless in His resources. There is no end, bottom, or ceiling to His riches. He can provide anything and everything a person needs from absolutely nothing. Consider just a few of the examples we are given in the Scriptures. Think of the two loaves of bread and five small fish that fed somewhere near 15,000 people. Consider the fish that was pulled from the water whose mouth held the money needed to pay the tax. Remember the jars of oil and flour that never ran out? Bread from heaven fell from the sky every day for two million people for forty years! Clearly, God does not need our "help." He can do it Himself. Yet, He invites us to join Him in what He is doing. He allows us to be a part of it. Why? Relationship. It is the same reason a child helps their dad. It is the same reason a dad asks for his child's help. Then, there is the relationship and all the blessings that come from it.

As you and I help meet the needs of others, we join our Father in His work. The fruits (or blessings) of a relationship are the result. The time together, the deepening of the relationship, and the joy over a job done are just to name a few. As we join Him, we are near to Him in a special way. As we give, we are led by Him in remarkable ways and blessed by Him in uncommon ways. These blessings are unique and are the result of working together with Him.

May you and I work hard, not to "have" everything we want, but so that we **"have something to give him who has need."** To do so is to "enter the garage" with our Father (if you will) and join Him in His work in the lives of others. The blessing will be all ours!

GRUMBLING TO GRATITUDE
DEVOTION #2 - JEANNIE YATES

When I hear that a pastor's sermon is on giving, my first response is often negative. "I do not want to hear another talk about tithing." "Can I just give God more of my time and call it good?" "This sermon really applies to that person over there; they have more money to give." Do not get me wrong, I love to give. I love searching for the best Christmas or birthday gifts to give each person in my family. I love seeing their faces light up when they open the carefully chosen gift. However, there seems to be a shift in my heart when it comes to giving *my* money to God.

Well, that is my problem: thinking that *my* money belongs to me. The Bible clearly says, **"Both riches and honor come from you, and you rule over all. In your hand are power and might, and in your hand it is to make great and to give strength to all. O Lord our God, all this abundance that we have provided for building you a house for your holy name comes from your hand and is all your own"** (1 Chronicles 29:12, 16). It all comes from Him (see also Deuteronomy 10:14; Psalm 24:1; Colossians 1:16). My ability to do my job and earn money comes from Him. My every breath and heartbeat comes from God alone. If I have a little, it comes from God; if I have an abundance, it comes from God. What I really need is a heart adjustment.

I have heard it said that grateful people are giving people. I like to think I am a pretty grateful person. I often say "thank you" when someone does something to serve or provide for me. I am even pretty good about writing thank-you notes after receiving birthday or Christmas gifts. I thank God for my family, the beautiful weather, and the food set before me, but my gratefulness often stops short when I begin to focus on what I am "lacking." It is almost impossible for me to be grateful when I am grumbling. Gratitude quickly flees, and discontentment sets in.

In Ephesians 5:15-20, we read, **"Look carefully then how you walk, not as unwise but as wise, making the best use of the time, because the days are evil. Therefore do not be foolish, but understand what the will of the Lord is…Be filled with the Spirit, addressing one another in psalms and hymns and spiritual songs, singing and making melody to the Lord with your heart, giving thanks always and for everything to God the Father in the name of our Lord Jesus Christ."** I love what the Bible commentator Kent Hughes says about these verses. He writes, "The fullness of the Spirit does call us to a radical spirit of gratitude… [it] rules out a grumbling, complaining, negative, sour spirit. No one can be Spirit-filled and traffic in these things. In America we, as a people, have so much. Yet, we characteristically mourn what we do not have: another's house, car, job, vacation, even family! Such thanklessness indicates a life missing the fullness of the Holy Spirit."

Only when I make that heart adjustment and focus my gaze on Jesus can I turn my grumbling into gratitude. Choosing to give thanks in all things and for all things changes my perspective and allows me to give, not out of obligation, but as an act of worship to my Savior.

In 2 Corinthians 9:7-8, we are told, **"Each one must give as he has decided in his heart, not reluctantly or under compulsion, for God loves a cheerful giver. And God is able to make all grace abound to you, so that having all sufficiency in all things at all times, you may abound in every good work."**

LIKENESS OF THE FATHER
DEVOTION #3 - DAVID HUDGENS

"Therefore be imitators of God, as beloved children. And walk in love, as Christ loved us and gave himself up for us, a fragrant offering and sacrifice to God." Ephesians 5:1-2

Some time ago, I was attending a building dedication ceremony for a newly completed substance abuse treatment and worship center. As a part of the ceremony, I was invited to share a special musical selection. After the dedication had ended, I was approached by a gentleman whom I did not know. The man introduced himself and then proceeded to ask me a question, "You are Dave's kid, aren't you?" (David was my father's first name as well.) I nodded yes, and he proceeded to explain to me just how quickly and easily, from my mannerisms, speech, and demonstrated passion for the Lord, he could tell that I was my father's son. At that moment, I did not think much of his words. Instead, I offered a polite "thank you" for having introduced himself, and then I soon parted ways with him.

Regretfully, now many years later, I understand just how wonderful a compliment the man had granted me. The true nature of his observances on that day really meant that there were many things, in his view, about me that mimicked my father. That is to say, I resembled my dad's likeness not only physically but also in word and character; outwardly, I mirrored the image of my "creator," if you will.

In Paul's letter to the church in Ephesus, he exhorts his audience to live in such a way as to be imitators of the Creator, God Himself. More specifically, he calls us to follow after Jesus' commitment to love sacrificially. In the sections before and after these two verses, Paul describes plainly what aroma should be produced from the life of one living for Jesus. Anyone who is committed to living in the newness of God should abstain from certain immoral behaviors and instead practice the holiness to which God has called us and equipped us to live in Christ.

As transformed children of God, our attitudes and actions should paint a portrait that resembles the holy, set-apart character and nature of God Himself. As such, we are to sacrifice our personal convictions and moral determinations to be burned upon the altar of God so that the purity and righteousness of God may take a supreme position in their place.

In other words, the believer is to live in such a way as to perhaps cause another to pause and ask, "You are God's kid, aren't you?"

A BOY'S LUNCH
DEVOTION #4 - JILL OSMON

Whenever we study about giving, my grandparents instantly come to my mind. They were not wealthy people (by the world's standards), but they were generous with their money, time, love, and wisdom. We automatically think of money when it comes to giving, and for good reason. The Bible is certainly clear about God's command to give of our money.

In today's culture, money is essential to living well. We cannot exist without money, but it is not the only way we are called to give. Ephesians 4:28 says, **"Let the thief no longer steal, but rather let him labor, doing honest work with his own hands, so that he may have something to share with anyone in need."** One of the most profound concepts that my grandparents taught us is that giving your time and resources produces an abundance. It is an abundance of love, empathy, opportunities to give the Gospel, and bringing God glory.

We see this in the life of Jesus. In John chapter 6, we find a small boy willing to give what he had (small in comparison to what was actually needed), and Jesus took it to provide for a multitude of people. John 6:1-14 records, **"After this Jesus went away to the other side of the Sea of Galilee, which is the Sea of Tiberias. And a large crowd was following him, because they saw the signs that he was doing on the sick. Jesus went up on the mountain, and there he sat down with his disciples. Now the Passover, the feast of the Jews, was at hand. Lifting up his eyes, then, and seeing that a large crowd was coming toward him, Jesus said to Philip, 'Where are we to buy bread, so that these people** *may eat?' He said this to test him, for he himself knew what he would do. Philip answered him, 'Two hundred denarii worth of bread would not be enough for each of them to get a little.' One of his disciples, Andrew, Simon Peter's brother, said to him, 'There is a boy here who has five barley loaves and two fish, but what are they for so many?' Jesus said, 'Have the people sit down.' Now there was much grass in the place. So the men sat down, about five thousand in number. Jesus then took the loaves, and when he had given thanks, he distributed them to those who were seated. So also the fish, as much as they wanted. And when they had eaten their fill, he told his disciples, 'Gather up the leftover fragments, that nothing may be lost.' So they gathered them up and filled twelve baskets with fragments from the five barley loaves left by those who had eaten. When the people saw the sign that he had done, they said, 'This is indeed the Prophet who is to come into the world!'"*

Jesus could have provided food for the crowd without the small boy's offering, but He offered up an opportunity for this small boy to give and see his gift be multiplied over and over again.

Our giving (whether money, resources, or time) may seem small in the larger picture of what others can offer, but we know that God will take our offerings and multiply them farther and greater than we could ever do on our own. However, it requires us to actually give. Do not compare your offering to others. It does not matter what they are giving; it only matters that we take what God has given us and offer it back to Him to use for His glory and the furtherance of the Gospel. If we decide to keep to ourselves what God has given us, we withhold from ourselves the blessing of being used by God.

What gift (big or small) do you have that you may be holding onto because you are comparing it to others or want to keep it for yourself? Let this be a challenge to you. Ask God to reveal to you the areas in your life where you need to give and the opportunities to put that into practice.

SMELL TEST
DEVOTION #5 - PASTOR CALEB COMBS

"Therefore be imitators of God, as beloved children. And walk in love, as Christ loved us and gave himself up for us, a fragrant offering and sacrifice to God." Ephesians 5:1-2

Have you ever done the smell test? I mean, have you ever taken a whiff of something on behalf of a friend? Jeff Foxworthy calls it a "courtesy smell" when you confirm, "Yes, it does smell like rotten eggs." I have a 15-year-old son whom I have had to teach about body odor. Yes, I do ask myself, "How can someone smell like that?" Some of us have better senses of smell than others, but let us not dwell on smelling bad; let us talk about something smelling good. What is the first thing that comes to mind when you think of something smelling good? For me, it is fresh chocolate chip cookies right out of the oven. It is so good!

Well, in Ephesians 5:1-2, Paul uses the phrase **"fragrant offering"** when referring to the sacrifice Jesus made. Now, what does that mean? Paul is addressing the church in Ephesus and referencing the Old Testament law of sacrifice. They would burn a sacrifice that smelled good to God. They would also burn incense in sacred places so that the aroma would reach the nostrils of God and please Him.

Paul begins the passage by telling us to be imitators of God, to walk in love as Christ loved and gave. Jesus gave up His life, as the Bible tells us, as a payment for many. John 15:13 tells us, **"Greater love has no one than this, that someone lay down his life for his friends."** Jesus gave up His life for you and me, and it smelled good to God. This concept might be somewhat mind-boggling, but what I

GIVING - 95

want to share with you is the concept of giving of oneself. Romans 12:1 echoes this concept by saying, ***"I appeal to you therefore, brothers, by the mercies of God, to present your bodies as a living sacrifice, holy and acceptable to God, which is your spiritual worship."***

We consistently see this concept of giving throughout Scripture. Some of you might have tuned out when I mentioned giving, but stick with me for a couple more minutes. God has called us, as His followers, to imitate Jesus in sacrificial giving. It includes giving our time, treasures, and talents. This "smells good" or pleases the Father. John chapter 3 says God loved us and gave, and 1 John says we love because He first loved us. Now, this may seem like a stretch, but I believe we give because He first gave to us. Being faithful in giving to a ministry or serving in a ministry follows the biblical example Jesus set for us. I encourage you to seek God and ask Him through prayer, "What am I holding back, and what should I be giving?" You will find out that God blesses the faithful giver in amazing ways far beyond earthly possessions. Malachi chapter 3 says He will pour out blessings in your life as we are faithful in giving, just as Jesus was.

THE GIFT OF SERVICE
DEVOTION #6 - PASTOR JUSTIN DEAN

Giving is a multifaceted area of the church that often gets labeled as purely financial. The early church deeply understood what it meant to provide for each other's needs financially and through service to one another. Living in a society motivated by money rather than services, we often forget the call to provide for the needs of the church according to our skills and time.

Look at Ephesians 6:7-8, **"Rendering service with a good will as to the Lord and not to man, knowing that whatever good anyone does, this he will receive back from the Lord, whether he is a bondservant or is free."**

The Greek for service here (douleuó) means to be subjected or devoted to. Our mindset should be on what or who we should be devoted to.

As believers, who or what are some things we should be devoted to?

I hope that one of your answers will be "to Christ" or "to God." This is a very true statement, but one of the ways that we demonstrate that we are devoted to Christ is through devotion to His Bride, the Church. We are called to provide service to one another, our brothers and sisters in Christ. This is not meant to be done out of guilt, sparingly, or with grumbling but out of heart desiring to offer that same service to the Lord Himself. Often, we treat Sunday morning gatherings like a concert that we simply pay for through our tithes. The Church is each one of us as believers, and we give financially to the institution, but we should also give in the ways in which we serve each other.

What are some skills that you have that you could offer to the Church?

Unfortunately, some people tend to use this as a substitute to avoid giving financially. We are called to submit both unto the Lord, our finances, and the skills with which He has blessed us. I would challenge you to reflect on your heart in regard to the giving of your finances and time to the Church. Do you give and serve as you would to the Lord, or do you do it with a heart of reluctance and grumbling?

James 2:15-16 reminds us, **"If a brother or sister is poorly clothed and lacking in daily food, and one of you says to them, 'Go in peace, be warmed and filled,' without giving them the things needed for the body, what good is that?"**

APPENDIX

THE BOOK OF EPHESIANS

EPHESIANS ONE
ENGLISH STANDARD VERSION

Greeting

¹ Paul, an apostle of Christ Jesus by the will of God,

To the saints who are in Ephesus, and are faithful in Christ Jesus:

² Grace to you and peace from God our Father and the Lord Jesus Christ.

Spiritual Blessings in Christ

³ Blessed be the God and Father of our Lord Jesus Christ, who has blessed us in Christ with every spiritual blessing in the heavenly places, ⁴ even as he chose us in him before the foundation of the world, that we should be holy and blameless before him. In love ⁵ he predestined us for adoption to himself as sons through Jesus Christ, according to the purpose of his will, ⁶ to the praise of his glorious grace, with which he has blessed us in the Beloved. ⁷ In him we have redemption through his blood, the forgiveness of our trespasses, according to the riches of his grace, ⁸ which he lavished upon us, in all wisdom and insight ⁹ making known to us the mystery of his will, according to his purpose, which he set forth in Christ ¹⁰ as a plan for the fullness of time, to unite all things in him, things in heaven and things on earth.

¹¹ In him we have obtained an inheritance, having been predestined according to the purpose of him who works all things according to the counsel of his will, ¹² so that we who were the first to hope in Christ might be to the praise of his glory. ¹³ In him you also,

when you heard the word of truth, the gospel of your salvation, and believed in him, were sealed with the promised Holy Spirit, [14] who is the guarantee of our inheritance until we acquire possession of it, to the praise of his glory.

Thanksgiving and Prayer

[15] For this reason, because I have heard of your faith in the Lord Jesus and your love toward all the saints, [16] I do not cease to give thanks for you, remembering you in my prayers, [17] that the God of our Lord Jesus Christ, the Father of glory, may give you the Spirit of wisdom and of revelation in the knowledge of him, [18] having the eyes of your hearts enlightened, that you may know what is the hope to which he has called you, what are the riches of his glorious inheritance in the saints, [19] and what is the immeasurable greatness of his power toward us who believe, according to the working of his great might [20] that he worked in Christ when he raised him from the dead and seated him at his right hand in the heavenly places, [21] far above all rule and authority and power and dominion, and above every name that is named, not only in this age but also in the one to come. [22] And he put all things under his feet and gave him as head over all things to the church, [23] which is his body, the fullness of him who fills all in all.

EPHESIANS TWO
ENGLISH STANDARD VERSION

By Grace Through Faith

[1] And you were dead in the trespasses and sins [2] in which you once walked, following the course of this world, following the prince of the power of the air, the spirit that is now at work in the sons of disobedience— [3] among whom we all once lived in the passions of our flesh, carrying out the desires of the body and the mind, and were by nature children of wrath, like the rest of mankind. [4] But God, being rich in mercy, because of the great love with which he loved us, [5] even when we were dead in our trespasses, made us alive together with Christ—by grace you have been saved— [6] and raised us up with him and seated us with him in the heavenly places in Christ Jesus, [7] so that in the coming ages he might show the immeasurable riches of his grace in kindness toward us in Christ Jesus. [8] For by grace you have been saved through faith. And this is not your own doing; it is the gift of God, [9] not a result of works, so that no one may boast. [10] For we are his workmanship, created in Christ Jesus for good works, which God prepared beforehand, that we should walk in them.

One in Christ

[11] Therefore remember that at one time you Gentiles in the flesh, called "the uncircumcision" by what is called the circumcision, which is made in the flesh by hands— [12] remember that you were at that time separated from Christ, alienated from the commonwealth of Israel and strangers to the covenants of promise, having no hope and without God in the world. [13] But now in Christ Jesus you who once

were far off have been brought near by the blood of Christ. [14] For he himself is our peace, who has made us both one and has broken down in his flesh the dividing wall of hostility [15] by abolishing the law of commandments expressed in ordinances, that he might create in himself one new man in place of the two, so making peace, [16] and might reconcile us both to God in one body through the cross, thereby killing the hostility. [17] And he came and preached peace to you who were far off and peace to those who were near. [18] For through him we both have access in one Spirit to the Father. [19] So then you are no longer strangers and aliens, but you are fellow citizens with the saints and members of the household of God, [20] built on the foundation of the apostles and prophets, Christ Jesus himself being the cornerstone, [21] in whom the whole structure, being joined together, grows into a holy temple in the Lord. [22] In him you also are being built together into a dwelling place for God by the Spirit.

EPHESIANS THREE
ENGLISH STANDARD VERSION

The Mystery of the Gospel Revealed

[1] For this reason I, Paul, a prisoner of Christ Jesus on behalf of you Gentiles— [2] assuming that you have heard of the stewardship of God's grace that was given to me for you, [3] how the mystery was made known to me by revelation, as I have written briefly. [4] When you read this, you can perceive my insight into the mystery of Christ, [5] which was not made known to the sons of men in other generations as it has now been revealed to his holy apostles and prophets by the Spirit. [6] This mystery is that the Gentiles are fellow heirs, members of the same body, and partakers of the promise in Christ Jesus through the gospel.

[7] Of this gospel I was made a minister according to the gift of God's grace, which was given me by the working of his power. [8] To me, though I am the very least of all the saints, this grace was given, to preach to the Gentiles the unsearchable riches of Christ, [9] and to bring to light for everyone what is the plan of the mystery hidden for ages in God, who created all things, [10] so that through the church the manifold wisdom of God might now be made known to the rulers and authorities in the heavenly places. [11] This was according to the eternal purpose that he has realized in Christ Jesus our Lord, [12] in whom we have boldness and access with confidence through our faith in him. [13] So I ask you not to lose heart over what I am suffering for you, which is your glory.

Prayer for Spiritual Strength

[14] For this reason I bow my knees before the Father, [15] from whom every family in heaven and on earth is named, [16] that according to the riches of his glory he may grant you to be strengthened with power through his Spirit in your inner being, [17] so that Christ may dwell in your hearts through faith—that you, being rooted and grounded in love, [18] may have strength to comprehend with all the saints what is the breadth and length and height and depth, [19] and to know the love of Christ that surpasses knowledge, that you may be filled with all the fullness of God.

[20] Now to him who is able to do far more abundantly than all that we ask or think, according to the power at work within us, [21] to him be glory in the church and in Christ Jesus throughout all generations, forever and ever. Amen.

EPHESIANS FOUR
ENGLISH STANDARD VERSION

Unity in the Body of Christ

¹ I therefore, a prisoner for the Lord, urge you to walk in a manner worthy of the calling to which you have been called, ² with all humility and gentleness, with patience, bearing with one another in love, ³ eager to maintain the unity of the Spirit in the bond of peace. ⁴ There is one body and one Spirit—just as you were called to the one hope that belongs to your call— ⁵ one Lord, one faith, one baptism, ⁶ one God and Father of all, who is over all and through all and in all. ⁷ But grace was given to each one of us according to the measure of Christ's gift. ⁸ Therefore it says,

"When he ascended on high he led a host of captives,
　and he gave gifts to men."

⁹ (In saying, "He ascended," what does it mean but that he had also descended into the lower regions, the earth? ¹⁰ He who descended is the one who also ascended far above all the heavens, that he might fill all things.) ¹¹ And he gave the apostles, the prophets, the evangelists, the shepherds and teachers, ¹² to equip the saints for the work of ministry, for building up the body of Christ, ¹³ until we all attain to the unity of the faith and of the knowledge of the Son of God, to mature manhood, to the measure of the stature of the fullness of Christ, ¹⁴ so that we may no longer be children, tossed to and fro by the waves and carried about by every wind of doctrine, by human cunning, by craftiness in deceitful schemes. ¹⁵ Rather, speaking the truth in love, we are to grow up in every way into him who is the head, into Christ, ¹⁶ from whom the whole body, joined and held together by every joint with which it is equipped, when each part is

working properly, makes the body grow so that it builds itself up in love.

The New Life

17 Now this I say and testify in the Lord, that you must no longer walk as the Gentiles do, in the futility of their minds. 18 They are darkened in their understanding, alienated from the life of God because of the ignorance that is in them, due to their hardness of heart. 19 They have become callous and have given themselves up to sensuality, greedy to practice every kind of impurity. 20 But that is not the way you learned Christ!— 21 assuming that you have heard about him and were taught in him, as the truth is in Jesus, 22 to put off your old self, which belongs to your former manner of life and is corrupt through deceitful desires, 23 and to be renewed in the spirit of your minds, 24 and to put on the new self, created after the likeness of God in true righteousness and holiness.

25 Therefore, having put away falsehood, let each one of you speak the truth with his neighbor, for we are members one of another. 26 Be angry and do not sin; do not let the sun go down on your anger, 27 and give no opportunity to the devil. 28 Let the thief no longer steal, but rather let him labor, doing honest work with his own hands, so that he may have something to share with anyone in need. 29 Let no corrupting talk come out of your mouths, but only such as is good for building up, as fits the occasion, that it may give grace to those who hear. 30 And do not grieve the Holy Spirit of God, by whom you were sealed for the day of redemption. 31 Let all bitterness and wrath and anger and clamor and slander be put away from you, along with all malice. 32 Be kind to one another, tenderhearted, forgiving one another, as God in Christ forgave you.

EPHESIANS FIVE
ENGLISH STANDARD VERSION

Walk in Love

¹ Therefore be imitators of God, as beloved children. ² And walk in love, as Christ loved us and gave himself up for us, a fragrant offering and sacrifice to God.

³ But sexual immorality and all impurity or covetousness must not even be named among you, as is proper among saints. ⁴ Let there be no filthiness nor foolish talk nor crude joking, which are out of place, but instead let there be thanksgiving. ⁵ For you may be sure of this, that everyone who is sexually immoral or impure, or who is covetous (that is, an idolater), has no inheritance in the kingdom of Christ and God. ⁶ Let no one deceive you with empty words, for because of these things the wrath of God comes upon the sons of disobedience. ⁷ Therefore do not become partners with them; ⁸ for at one time you were darkness, but now you are light in the Lord. Walk as children of light ⁹ (for the fruit of light is found in all that is good and right and true), ¹⁰ and try to discern what is pleasing to the Lord. ¹¹ Take no part in the unfruitful works of darkness, but instead expose them. ¹² For it is shameful even to speak of the things that they do in secret. ¹³ But when anything is exposed by the light, it becomes visible, ¹⁴ for anything that becomes visible is light. Therefore it says,

> "Awake, O sleeper,
>   and arise from the dead,
>   and Christ will shine on you."

¹⁵ Look carefully then how you walk, not as unwise but as wise, ¹⁶ making the best use of the time, because the days are

evil. [17] Therefore do not be foolish, but understand what the will of the Lord is. [18] And do not get drunk with wine, for that is debauchery, but be filled with the Spirit, [19] addressing one another in psalms and hymns and spiritual songs, singing and making melody to the Lord with your heart, [20] giving thanks always and for everything to God the Father in the name of our Lord Jesus Christ, [21] submitting to one another out of reverence for Christ.

Wives and Husbands

[22] Wives, submit to your own husbands, as to the Lord. [23] For the husband is the head of the wife even as Christ is the head of the church, his body, and is himself its Savior. [24] Now as the church submits to Christ, so also wives should submit in everything to their husbands.

[25] Husbands, love your wives, as Christ loved the church and gave himself up for her, [26] that he might sanctify her, having cleansed her by the washing of water with the word, [27] so that he might present the church to himself in splendor, without spot or wrinkle or any such thing, that she might be holy and without blemish. [28] In the same way husbands should love their wives as their own bodies. He who loves his wife loves himself. [29] For no one ever hated his own flesh, but nourishes and cherishes it, just as Christ does the church, [30] because we are members of his body. [31] "Therefore a man shall leave his father and mother and hold fast to his wife, and the two shall become one flesh." [32] This mystery is profound, and I am saying that it refers to Christ and the church. [33] However, let each one of you love his wife as himself, and let the wife see that she respects her husband.

EPHESIANS SIX
ENGLISH STANDARD VERSION

Children and Parents

¹ Children, obey your parents in the Lord, for this is right. ² "Honor your father and mother" (this is the first commandment with a promise), ³ "that it may go well with you and that you may live long in the land." ⁴ Fathers, do not provoke your children to anger, but bring them up in the discipline and instruction of the Lord.

Bondservants and Masters

⁵ Bondservants, obey your earthly masters with fear and trembling, with a sincere heart, as you would Christ, ⁶ not by the way of eye-service, as people-pleasers, but as bondservants of Christ, doing the will of God from the heart, ⁷ rendering service with a good will as to the Lord and not to man, ⁸ knowing that whatever good anyone does, this he will receive back from the Lord, whether he is a bondservant or is free. ⁹ Masters, do the same to them, and stop your threatening, knowing that he who is both their Master and yours is in heaven, and that there is no partiality with him.

The Whole Armor of God

¹⁰ Finally, be strong in the Lord and in the strength of his might. ¹¹ Put on the whole armor of God, that you may be able to stand against the schemes of the devil. ¹² For we do not wrestle against flesh and blood, but against the rulers, against the authorities, against the cosmic powers over this present darkness, against the spiritual forces of evil in the heavenly places. ¹³ Therefore take up the whole armor of

God, that you may be able to withstand in the evil day, and having done all, to stand firm. [14] Stand therefore, having fastened on the belt of truth, and having put on the breastplate of righteousness, [15] and, as shoes for your feet, having put on the readiness given by the gospel of peace. [16] In all circumstances take up the shield of faith, with which you can extinguish all the flaming darts of the evil one; [17] and take the helmet of salvation, and the sword of the Spirit, which is the word of God, [18] praying at all times in the Spirit, with all prayer and supplication. To that end, keep alert with all perseverance, making supplication for all the saints, [19] and also for me, that words may be given to me in opening my mouth boldly to proclaim the mystery of the gospel, [20] for which I am an ambassador in chains, that I may declare it boldly, as I ought to speak.

Final Greetings

[21] So that you also may know how I am and what I am doing, Tychicus the beloved brother and faithful minister in the Lord will tell you everything. [22] I have sent him to you for this very purpose, that you may know how we are, and that he may encourage your hearts.

[23] Peace be to the brothers, and love with faith, from God the Father and the Lord Jesus Christ. [24] Grace be with all who love our Lord Jesus Christ with love incorruptible.

OUR VISION

Matthew 28:19-20: *"Go therefore and make disciples of all nations, baptizing them in the name of the Father and of the Son and of the Holy Spirit, teaching them to observe all that I have commanded you. And behold, I am with you always, to the end of the age."*

REACH

At The River Church, you will often hear the phrase, "We don't go to church, we are the Church." We believe that as God's people, our primary purpose and goal is to go out and make disciples of Jesus Christ. We encourage you to reach the world in your local communities.

GATHER

The goal of weekend gatherings at The River Church is to glorify Christ in all we do! Whether it be through singing, giving, serving, or any of the variety of ways He has gifted us and called us together, Jesus is at the center of it all. We celebrate that when followers of Christ gather together in unity, it's not only a refresher, it brings life-change!

GROW

Our Growth Communities are designed to mirror the early church in Acts as having *"all things in common."* They are smaller collections of believers who spend time together studying the Word, knowing and caring for one another relationally, and learning to increase their commitment to Christ by holding one another accountable.

The River Church
8393 E. Holly Rd.
Holly, MI 48442

theriverchurch.cc • info@theriverchurch.cc

Made in the USA
Columbia, SC
01 December 2024